IF FOUND PI

👤 _____

✉ _____

📱 _____

Greater Than a Tourist Book Series Reviews from Readers

I think the series is wonderful and beneficial for tourists to get information before visiting the city.

-Seckin Zumbul, Izmir Turkey

I am a world traveler who has read many trip guides but this one really made a difference for me. I would call it a heartfelt creation of a local guide expert instead of just a guide.

-Susy, Isla Holbox, Mexico

New to the area like me, this is a must have!

-Joe, Bloomington, USA

This is a good series that gets down to it when looking for things to do at your destination without having to read a novel for just a few ideas.

-Rachel, Monterey, USA

Good information to have to plan my trip to this destination.

-Pennie Farrell, Mexico

Great ideas for a port day.

-Mary Martin USA

Aptly titled, you won't just be a tourist after reading this book. You'll be greater than a tourist!

-Alan Warner, Grand Rapids, USA

Even though I only have three days to spend in San Miguel in an upcoming visit, I will use the author's suggestions to guide some of my time there. An easy read - with chapters named to guide me in directions I want to go.

-Robert Catapano, USA

Great insights from a local perspective! Useful information and a very good value!

-Sarah, USA

This series provides an in-depth experience through the eyes of a local. Reading these series will help you to travel the city in with confidence and it'll make your journey a unique one.

-Andrew Teoh, Ipoh, Malaysia

>TOURIST

GREATER THAN A TOURIST- TENNESSEE USA

50 Travel Tips from a Local

Kirsten Marrs

Greater Than a Tourist- Tennessee USA   Copyright © 2018 by CZYK Publishing LLC. All Rights Reserved.

All rights reserved. No part of this book may be reproduced in any form or by any electronic or mechanical means including information storage and retrieval systems, without permission in writing from the author. The only exception is by a reviewer, who may quote short excerpts in a review.

Cover designed by: Ivana Stamenkovic
Cover Image: https://pixabay.com/en/tennessee-landscape-mountains-trees-69001/

CZYK Publishing Since 2011.

Greater Than a Tourist
Visit our website at www.GreaterThanaTourist.com

Lock Haven, PA
All rights reserved.
ISBN: 9781723980831

>TOURIST

50 TRAVEL TIPS FROM A LOCAL

\>TOURIST

BOOK DESCRIPTION

Are you excited about planning your next trip?

Do you want to try something new?

Would you like some guidance from a local?

If you answered yes to any of these questions, then this Greater Than a Tourist book is for you.

Greater Than a Tourist- Tennessee by Kirsten Marrs offers the inside scoop on Tennessee. Most travel books tell you how to travel like a tourist. Although there is nothing wrong with that, as part of the Greater Than a Tourist series, this book will give you travel tips from someone who has lived at your next travel destination.

In these pages, you will discover advice that will help you throughout your stay. This book will not tell you exact addresses or store hours but instead will give you excitement and knowledge from a local that you may not find in other smaller print travel books.

Travel like a local. Slow down, stay in one place, and get to know the people and the culture. By the time you finish this book, you will be eager and prepared to travel to your next destination.

TABLE OF CONTENTS

BOOK DESCRIPTION
TABLE OF CONTENTS
DEDICATION
ABOUT THE AUTHOR
HOW TO USE THIS BOOK
FROM THE PUBLISHER
OUR STORY
WELCOME TO
> TOURIST
INTRODUCTION
1. NASHVILLE, the "Music City"
2. HISTORIC RUGBY, a Utopian dream
3. CHATTANOOGA, The Scenic City
4. MEMPHIS, TN, a city of "Grit and Grind"
5. DAYTON, home of the Scopes Trial
6. BELL BUCKLE, a walk through history
7. THE CHEROHALA SKYWAY, a National Scenic Byway
8. CADES COVE
9. OAK RIDGE, "The Secret City"
10. VONORE, Sequoyah Birthplace Museum
11. DOLLYWOOD
12. GATLINBURG, the Mountain Resort City
13. ROCK CITY, See the Seven States

14. DUNLAP, a Hang-glider's Dream
15. LYNCHBURG, Home of the Jack Daniels Distillery
16. PARIS, Home of the World's Biggest Fish Fry
17. THE LOST SEA ADVENTURES, America's Largest Underground Lake
18. RUBY FALLS, Naturally wonderful
19. FALL CREEK FALLS STATE PARK
20. FROZEN HEAD STATE PARK
21. COSBY CAMPGROUND
22. INDIAN BOUNDARY
23. WHITE WATER RAFTING ON THE OCOEE
24. CROSSVILLE, The Golf Capital of Tennessee
25. CHICKAMAUGA AND CHATTANOOGA NATIONAL MILITARY PARK
26. CARTER HOUSE & CARNTON, Franklin, TN
27. FORT PILLOW STATE PARK, Henning
28. KNOXVILLE, The Heart and Soul of East Tennessee
29. BRISTOL, Home of the Bristol Motor Speedway
30. SUNNY SIDE TRAIL
31. KINGSPORT
32. JOHNSON CITY
33. AUDUBON ACRES, Chattanooga
34. ANDREW JACKSON'S HERMITAGE, Nashville

\>TOURIST

35. GAYLORD OPRYLAND HOTEL, Nashville
36. THE CAVERNS "PERFORMANCE HALL," Pelham
37. CUMBERLAND CAVERNS
38. GRACELAND MANSION
39. ELKMONT CAMPGROUND
40. THE BELL WITCH CAVE
41. VIRGIN FALLS POCKET WILDERNESS
42. CASEY JONES VILLAGE
43. INTERNATIONAL TOWING AND RECOVERY MUSEUM
44. PRESIDENT JAMES K. POLK TOMB
45. BILLY TRIPP'S MINDFIELD
46. PINSON MOUNDS STATE ARCHEOLOGICAL PARK
47. LOOKOUT MOUNTAIN INCLINE RAILWAY
48. BACKYARD TERROR'S DINOSAUR PARK
49. NATIONAL CIVIL RIGHTS MUSEUM
50. CONCRETE PARTHENON

TOP REASONS TO BOOK THIS TRIP
50 THINGS TO KNOW ABOUT PACKING LIGHT FOR TRAVEL
Packing and Planning Tips
Travel Questions
Travel Bucket List
NOTES

DEDICATION

This book is dedicated to the beauty of Tennessee and all who have contributed to its history and continued growth and preservation.

ABOUT THE AUTHOR

Kirsten is a freelance writer and former teacher who lives in Chattanooga, TN. She loves to be outdoors, travel, read, and to be a mother to her two (soon three) children.

Kirsten loves to travel anywhere and everywhere, whether it is ten miles down the road or three hundred.

Kirsten spent most of her adolescent years in Spring City, TN, attended college at Middle Tennessee State University in Murfreesboro, TN, and now resides in Chattanooga, TN.

HOW TO USE THIS BOOK

The Greater Than a Tourist book series was written by someone who has lived in an area for over three months. The goal of this book is to help travelers either dream or experience different locations by providing opinions from a local. The author has made suggestions based on their own experiences. Please do your own research before traveling to the area in case the suggested places are unavailable.

>TOURIST

FROM THE PUBLISHER

Traveling can be one of the most important parts of a person's life. The anticipation and memories that you have are some of the best. As a publisher of the Greater Than a Tourist book series, as well as the popular 50 Things to Know book series, we strive to help you learn about new places, spark your imagination, and inspire you. Wherever you are and whatever you do I wish you safe, fun, and inspiring travel.

Lisa Rusczyk Ed. D.
CZYK Publishing

OUR STORY

Traveling is a passion of the "Greater than a Tourist" series creator. Lisa studied abroad in college, and for their honeymoon Lisa and her husband toured Europe. During her travels to Malta, an older man tried to give her some advice based on his own experience living on the island since he was a young boy. She was not sure if she should talk to the stranger but was interested in his advice. When traveling to some places she was wary to talk to locals because she was afraid that they weren't being genuine. Through her travels, Lisa learned how much locals had to share with tourists. Lisa created the "Greater Than a Tourist" book series to help connect people with locals. A topic that locals are very passionate about sharing.

>TOURIST

```
WELCOME TO
> TOURIST
```

INTRODUCTION

"Every traveler has a home of his own and he learns to appreciate it the more from his wandering."

-Charles Dickens

The Great Smoky Mountains. TVA. Sweet tea. "Bless your heart." Southern hospitality. Rocky Top. These strike a chord when you think of Tennessee. Tennessee's beauty will captivate you and have you humming a sweet, slow country song before you know it. That Southern drawl you'll hear will keep you hanging on every word. If you are looking for a sweet, slower pace, then visiting Tennessee should be next on your travel bucket list. Tennessee culture has you outdoors more often than not as you enjoy the natural beauty, so there are many options for camping and outdoor activities in this tour guide. As a native to Tennessee, anytime I travel out of state, there is never more pride than when I cross back over that Tennessee state line and see our beautiful mountains and evergreens. Growing up in Tennessee is something I am thankful for. I went to a very small combined elementary and middle school, then called

Spring City Elementary School. That school was the only school in Spring City at the time. We had our marching band, football teams, and all the other sports teams and we all got along just fine. From there, there is only one high school which the whole county feeds into: Rhea County High School. I consider myself lucky to have gone through a school in which there was no choice as to which school you went to; upper, middle, and low class families all worked together and we made quite the team. I never planned, and still have not planned even though I am into my 30s, moving from this beautiful state. I am also quite partial to Chattanooga since I have spent most of my adult life here. I hope that you are able to experience the joy, sweetness, beauty, and hospitality the way I see it. Enjoy planning your visit to Tennessee- "America at Its Best".

>TOURIST

1. NASHVILLE, THE "MUSIC CITY"

Start your trip in the middle of Tennessee at the state's capital! If you are looking for the music scene, you can visit the Ryman Auditorium, otherwise known as the "Mother Church of Country Music". My first concert at the Ryman was Old Crow Medicine Show, and I remember just being ecstatic at the beauty of the venue and the acoustics. Or, head down Music Row on 16th and 17th Avenue South. Nightlife abounds down the famous Ryman Alley. Are you looking for historical venues? Purchase your tickets and swing by The Hermitage, President Jackson's mansion-turned-museum. Possibly take a tour of the Belle Meade Plantation, an 1840s plantation home with a winery. For some delicious dining, check out Monell's Dining and Catering, The Loveless Cafe, Hattie B's Hot Chicken, Lockeland Table, 417 Union, Flyte World Dining and Wine, and so many more. The sampling of fantastic foods that will have your tastebuds singing seem to be around every corner in Nashville. You really cannot go wrong choosing one of the local spots to eat.

2. HISTORIC RUGBY, A UTOPIAN DREAM

Meander through the tall pines and oaks as you walk the Utopian dream town of Thomas Hughes' 1880 dream of a perfect society. The Utopian society lasted until roughly 1900, but with much difficulty along the way. Stop by and experience the village with friendly volunteers and staff. I first visited Rugby when I was in grade school and adored the village then; I was a big "Little House on the Prairie" fan and loved any history around that time frame. I also enjoy visiting now as an adult and marveling at the effort of the small town. The only restaurant you will find in Rugby is the Harrow Road Cafe, but it is quite the find with some down-home cooking and sweets.

3. CHATTANOOGA, THE SCENIC CITY

Known as The Scenic City, you will find no shortage of outdoor activities. Check out the Volkswagen Enterprise South Nature Park for hiking, biking, horse trails, or just a beautiful drive through nature. You will also find plenty of options for paddleboarding, kayaking, or boating while you visit. Stop by the Tennessee Aquarium, known for its iconic skyline view of the triangular glass spires. The Tennessee Aquarium;s first building is River Journey, an entire building dedicated to freshwater animals and life, featuring the Cove Forest which is the only indoor forest to naturally go through all four seasons. The second building, Ocean Journey, was recently constructed and hosts oceanic animals and life. For beautiful Fall foliage, try visiting in the Autumn months. For those of you who love shopping, walking, and great food, head downtown to the Walnut Street Bridge for a stroll on the beautiful walking bridge, one of the longest pedestrian bridges in the world, which takes you to many fun, quirky shops and local cuisine. Some restaurants not to miss include: locally owned and operated Terminal Brewhouse, Stir, The Chattanooga Choo Choo, Polly Claire's Teahouse, The Hot Chocolatier, Big River Grille and Brewing Works, The Public House, The Boathouse, St. John's, The Meeting Place, The 24-hour City Cafe, and The Pickle Barrel. That was quite an extensive list of restaurants, but they are all too good not to mention. Those restaurants will keep your tastebuds happy all around Chattanooga. There is no shortage of that Southern Hospitality in Chattanooga, so enjoy your time being pampered with our sweet, Southern drawl.

4. MEMPHIS, TN, A CITY OF "GRIT AND GRIND"

Memphis adopted their motto "Grit and Grind" from their NBA team, The Grizzlies. Memphians have a lot of pride in the city especially when it come to music, food, and community. Memphis is the place to go for awesome barbecue, where there seems to be a barbecue place on every corner; the city even hosts the World Championship Barbecue Contest held during the Memphis in May celebration. Memphis is best known as the home of the blues. Go to Beale Street on any given night and you will find blues music somewhere. Check out the Stax Museum for some soul music history. As big as blues and soul are, Elvis probably takes the cake. People come from all over the world to visit Graceland and see Sun Studio. Make it in August for Elvis Week if you are an Elvis fan! Last, but not least, check out some free fun at the Peabody Hotel and see the famous Peabody Ducks. Have you ever wanted to walk the entirety of the Mississippi River? Well, you can now do just that at the Mud Island River Park. This park is a 5 block long replica of The Mississippi River, and you can walk the whole 1.000 mile journey in those five blocks. Each 30" stride is equal to one mile of actual river. Along the way, you will be treated to the history of the land and river and learn about geographical features. Visit this park from April until it closes for the winter. Specific BBQ must visits include: Rendezvous, Central BBQ, Payne's, or Cozy Corner. Don't let the looks fool you; some of these are hole-in-the-wall eateries, but serve the best Memphis BBQ you will ever taste.

5. DAYTON, HOME OF THE SCOPES TRIAL

Dayton is a quaint town located between Chattanooga and Knoxville. I spent a lot of my younger days in Dayton, being as my hometown of Spring City was just twenty minutes away. The small city has grown up by renovating many of its downtown buildings and adding more unique eateries. For a laid-back day, walk around the downtown area and visit some of the local antique shops and restaurants. Stop by the courthouse downtown to see where the famous Scopes Trial was staged. Dayton is most famous for this "Scopes Monkey Trial" in which a local teacher in July of 1925, John T. Scopes, went to trial for teaching human evolution in a state-funded school, which was unlawful. The bottom line was, though, that the trial was staged in order to bring publicity to the small town and to the controversial issue itself. You can visit in July and be a part of the history during the Scopes Festival where you can watch a reenactment of the trial amongst other festivities. Where should you eat when you visit? Try Monkey Town Brewing Company; their local brews are mouth-watering and their food is such a surprise to the tastebuds with their unique pairings. Any time we drive through Dayton, we make sure to stop there. Another great local hot spot to eat is Jacob Myers Restaurant on the River. Last, but not least, try out the Screen Door Kitchen featuring all scratch-made meals including lowcountry specialties, Sunday brunch, burgers, and desserts.

>TOURIST

6. BELL BUCKLE, A WALK THROUGH HISTORY

If you are interested in a well-preserved piece of history, head on over to Bell Buckle. This small town is a perfectly preserved railroad town with beautiful Victorian homes and churches. Antiques, county music, home cooking, and Southern hospitality abound in Bell Buckle. I have fond memories of visiting Bell Buckle when I was younger, and have always enjoyed the town. Visit in June to enjoy the RC-Moon Pie Festival, a celebration of the original Southern fast food: an ice-cold RC cola and a fresh Moon Pie. For your tastebuds' delight, try any of the Bell Buckle Cafe or 82 American Diner.

7. THE CHEROHALA SKYWAY, A NATIONAL SCENIC BYWAY

For over forty miles of breathtaking views, take a drive on the Cherohala Skyway, a designated National Scenic Byway which connects the Cherokee National Forest in Tennessee to the Nantahala

National Forest in North Carolina. The elevations range from 900 feet above sea level to over 5,400 feet above sea level. I have childhood memories of driving the Cherohala Skyway with my parents for a sweet Sunday get-away in our own home state. Not far from the Cherohala Skyway Visitor Center are quite a few restaurants worth the stop: Tellico Grains, Tellicafe, Town Square Cafe, and The Cotton Pickin' Inn.

8. CADES COVE

As a child, I remember being excited to take a drive through Cades Cove. Cades Cove is a beautiful valley located in the Smoky Mountains. Offering numerous opportunities to see wildlife in the eleven mile driveable loop. Wildlife abounds in this verdant valley, with black bears being a common sight! Allow yourself two to four hours to complete this visit, especially if you park and walk some of the nature trails. Take a walk to the upper loop and see beautifully restored historical buildings including a working grist mill. Biking, hiking, a leisurely drive, and camping are all available at Cades Cove.

>TOURIST

9. OAK RIDGE, "THE SECRET CITY"

Oak Ridge was established in 1942 by the US government as a home base for the Manhattan Project, which was a secret project to produce the first US nuclear weapon. This town had everything anyone could want, including a swimming pool, a bar, a library, and a movie theater, but you had to pay the price of extreme secrecy to work and reside there. You can get a guided tour by the American Museum of Science and Energy through the Secret City of Oak Ridge. Visit in June for the Secret City Festival, complete with WWII reenactments. You can schedule your visit to the Oak Ridge National Laboratory, which is still in use. Before you visit, consider reading <u>Atomic City Girls</u> by Janet Beard for a very accurate historical fiction retelling of the life that Oak Ridge residents lived. Be sure to stop by one of these restaurants for some highly-recommended local eats: Dean's Restaurant and Bakery, Aubrey's, The Other One, or The Soup Kitchen.

10. VONORE, SEQUOYAH BIRTHPLACE MUSEUM

Take a trip to Vonore, TN to see the Sequoyah Birthplace Museum where you will get to walk through the life of the creator of the Cherokee alphabet. Plan your trip in September to experience the Cherokee Fall Festival. You will enjoy a beautiful drive there, as it is located in the Great Smoky Mountains of East Tennessee. My daughter took a field trip here and we all really enjoyed it. Great employees who really know their facts. While there are not many restaurants in Vonore, there are a few good ones worth mentioning: The Bay Bistro, Countryside, Genovese's Pizza, and Pizzaria Venti.

11. DOLLYWOOD

If you are a theme park junkie and love the down-home feel of the country, then a visit to Dollywood must be on your itinerary. Located in the metroplex of Pigeon Forge and spanning 150 acres of the Great Smoky Mountains, there are forty world-class rides along with fantastic entertainment sprinkled all throughout the park. Arrive early and plan to stay all day to enjoy some of the park's greatest dining experiences. For a taste explosion, you must stop by the Grist Mill located inside the park for their famous cinnamon bread. My favorite memories of Dollywood are the different types of shows you can indulge in while strolling around the park. Dollywood is a mini vacation spot for Tennesseans, but attracts many visitors as well. A unique vibe to this theme park is the fact that it is constructed in the mountains, so there is abundant nature surrounding and throughout the park. Adults will love The Wild Eagle roller coaster for some fun thrills, but there are plenty of kid-friendly rides as well. Check out these two kid favorites: The Mystery Mine and The Fire Chaser. Autumn and Winter are some of the best times to visit if you want to see exquisite decorations and the awe-inspiring Fall foliage. Summer time is a blast when you can also visit Dollywood's Splash Country. On your way to Dollywood, or while you are driving away, stop by The Mill for some fantastic food and shopping, or eat at Paula Deen's restaurant. You could also stop at one of the many famous pancake places!

12. GATLINBURG, THE MOUNTAIN RESORT CITY

Whether you seek skiing, shopping, eating, hiking, sightseeing, thrills, or rest, Gatlinburg can quench that for you. There's Ober Gatlinburg, featuring 9 runs and equipment rentals amongst other fun things to do. If skiing is not in your plans, there are Civil War reenactments galore. Be sure to pack your walking shoes as you walk the main strip where you will find attractions for anyone: shopping, Ripley's Aquarium of the Smokies, The Guiness World Book of Records Museum, Ripley's Believe It or Not Museum, the Gatlinburg SkyLift, old time photo shops, rides, putt-putt golf, candy stores, and arcades. Even natives of Tennessee flock to Gatlinburg, often at least once a year. There is just something about the sights and smells of a bustling, active city that keeps bringing us back. I grew up visiting Gatlinburg since before I can remember. My parents even had their honeymoon there over forty years ago before it was as busy as it is now! A great time to visit, as seems to be a theme, is the holiday season November through February when the city lines its streets with lights and decorations galore. It is common for Tennesseans to make a day trip just to drive up and down the strip looking at the lights. Some must visit restaurants include (but not limited to): Crocketts Breakfast Camp, Buckhorn Inn, Wild Plum Tearoom, and Log Cabin Pancake House.

13. ROCK CITY, SEE THE SEVEN STATES

Where else can you see seven states from one spot? When you visit Rock City, located on Lookout Mountain, six miles from downtown Chattanooga, you will be able to stop for a breathtaking panoramic view where you can see seven states: Tennessee, Kentucky, Virginia, North Carolina, South Carolina, Georgia, and Alabama. That is not the only thing the majestic Rock City has to offer: there are massive ancient rock formations, gardens hosting over 400 native plants, caverns, natural wonders, and local art. Have fun squeezing through Fat Man's squeeze and the Needle's Eye, but if the close quarters give you the heebie-jeebies, there is a way around them. There are many times throughout the year when there are special events that take place at Rock City. You can go Memorial Day through Labor Day to hear Summer Music Nights amid the beautiful star-studded night sky, see the Rock City Raptors (birds of prey) seasonally, Roctoberfest on October weekends (Rock City's version of Oktoberfest fun), Enchanted Garden of Lights November through December 31st, Shamrock City in March for the annual Irish festival, Fairytale Nights during March and April where all of your favorite fairytale dreams come to life, Earthdayz in April, and the Southern Blooms Festival in May where you can see all the native plants and enchanted gardens bloom to life. My favorite event is the Enchanted Garden of Lights which runs from November through January. My favorite thing to do at Rock City is to grab a Starbucks from the store which is located right outside of Rock City and stroll through the Enchanted Garden of Lights; it has become a winter tradition for my family.

>TOURIST

14. DUNLAP, A HANG-GLIDER'S DREAM

Looking for a thrill? Visit the Tennessee Tree Toppers at the Henson Gap launch site for hang-gliders located just off of Highway 111. This launch site provides a 160 foot vertical drop with numerous landing zones. The launch area provides camping, running water, and restrooms for a comfortable stay. If sticking to the water is more your thing, you can always canoe the Sequatchie river! After your thrills, you could complete your stay in Dunlap by visiting the Dunlap Coke Ovens and Museum, which houses the history of the town's coal mining heritage. If you happen to plan your trip in August, you could take part in the Highway 127 World's Longest Yard Sale which runs through Dunlap on its 675 mile spread! My favorite part about Dunlap is the drive from Chattanooga to Dunlap on highway 111; it is always a breath-taking view. I sometimes pull off at the scenic overlook and watch the hang-gliders soar their way through the sky. For some terrific views of the hills and the valleys, you must eat at The Cookie Jar; their homecooking is enough to bring you back time and again.

15. LYNCHBURG, HOME OF THE JACK DANIELS DISTILLERY

Have you always wondered how whiskey was distilled? Check out the Jack Daniels Distillery for multiple options of tours and tastings to find out that answer! I visited once on a chilly November day, but kept warm and toasty by their ovens which are used for their distilling process. When you are finished with your tour, head on over to Miss Mary Bobo's Boarding House and Restaurant for some down-home cooking. A few other recommended restaurants to try would be Lynchburg Fix'ns and Barrelhouse BBQ. Not done tasting whiskey? Head over to the Lynchburg Distillery for some more fun spirits.

16. PARIS, HOME OF THE WORLD'S BIGGEST FISH FRY

For a down-home feel, plan your visit to Paris in April for the annual all-you-can-eat catfish meal, complete with a parade, carnival, races, arts and crafts, rodeos, and dances. You can't miss their welcome sign to the city: a great big catfish perches atop the wooden welcome sign! But, a catfish fry isn't all you would visit Paris for; their restored downtown offers a 1920s feel with over forty shops to peruse. For good eats, check out: Southside Cafe, Ann & Dave's Kitchen, or Trolinger's. There is even a great photo op of a towercrop built as a replica of the Eiffel Tower. You can tell everyone you visited Paris...Tennessee!

17. THE LOST SEA ADVENTURES, AMERICA'S LARGEST UNDERGROUND LAKE

Located in beautiful Sweetwater, TN, the Lost Sea is America's largest underground lake. Your visit would consist of a ¾ mile round-trip cavern tour, with a glass-bottomed boat ride in the underground lake! You could end your visit enjoying a meal at the Cavern Kitchen followed up with some ice cream at their Ice Cream Parlor. Grown ups and kids alike get a kick out of the glass-bottomed boats where you will see humongous trout swimming beneath you. If you happen to be visiting Sweetwater on the weekend, swing by the Sweetwater Flea Market for fun, unusual souvenirs and treats.

18. RUBY FALLS, NATURALLY WONDERFUL

Visit the nation's largest and deepest waterfall open to the public on this stop in Chattanooga! There are three different experiences you can choose from: the classic waterfall tour, the lantern tour, or the extended cavern experience. My favorite part of the tour was hearing the history of how the falls were discovered. If you haven't had enough fun with the caverns and falls, you could fly on over to the Ruby Falls ZIPstream aerial adventures zip line course.

19. FALL CREEK FALLS STATE PARK

Fall Creek Falls State Park is one of Tennessee's most exquisite places to view our beautiful part of the world. The state park offers 222 standard and premium campsites, 16 primitive sites, and three backcountry sites. From the campground, you can walk or drive to the head of a trail that will take you to Fall Creek Falls, one of the highest waterfalls in the eastern United States, cascading 265 feet down. There is something for every style of outdoor adventurer at this state park, with more than 35 miles of hiking trails and 24 miles of mountain biking trails winding through the park. There is even an 18- hole golf course, a pool, a zipline course, and a sweet little shopping village to visit while you're there. My family visits Fall Creek Falls at least six times a year, all throughout the year, and we never get tired of its beauty.

20. FROZEN HEAD STATE PARK

Craving solitude and natural beauty? Head out to Frozen Head State Park. No bells and whistles here, just nature at its finest. This state park offers just 20 campsites spread widely through the Big Cove Campground. There are 50 miles of backpacking and hiking trails over the 24,000 acres. Each trail offers its own beauty; waterfalls, wildlife, and breathtaking views. You could come back over and over and see a new stretch of beauty each time. My family has been three times and we still have not been on the same trail twice!

21. COSBY CAMPGROUND

Located just 20 miles from Gatlinburg, this campground is a must if you want to live an adventurer's life but still have the big city close enough at hand for adventures of a different sort! Cosby campground hosts 157 campsites with access to the Appalachian Trail amongst many other trails. If you are an Appalachian Trail junkie, you might like to know that Tennessee has 94 miles of the AT, and an additional 160 miles along the Tennessee/ North Carolina borders.

22. INDIAN BOUNDARY

Located just two miles off of the Cherohala Skyway and part of the Cherokee National Forest, Indian Boundary offers 87 campsites. The swim beach has an exquisite view as it is nestled between towering rock walls and forest. The area has great sites to see as you enter the campground and lots of exploring to do. Our family makes a trip to Indian Boundary at least once every year, usually during the summer months so we can enjoy that beautiful swimming area. Some of my favorite memories of this campground are exploring the historical buildings on the way into the park, hiking the precarious trail down to the river, and swimming in that beautiful swimming hole.

23. WHITE WATER RAFTING ON THE OCOEE

Up for a thrill? How about a thrill on Olympic Class white water rapids? Check out any of the numerous companies who offer white water rafting on the Ocoee, the site of white water events in the 1996 Atlanta Olympic Games. Most companies offer guided trips lasting five miles to ten miles down the river. When I took my trip down the Ocoee, I remember feeling so apprehensive, but before you knew it, you were flying down the rapids and handling them like a pro! This river has the most continuous stretch of class III and class IV rapids out of any of the rivers in the country; this is sure to add some thrill to your vacation! Since you will have worked up an appetite, check out one of these nearby restaurants: The Paddler Cafe, Apricot Place Cafe, Bear's Den BBQ, or Ocoee Dam Deli and Diner.

24. CROSSVILLE, THE GOLF CAPITAL OF TENNESSEE

Crossville is nestled at the top of Tennessee's Cumberland Plateau and boasts of being The Golf Capital of Tennessee because it offers ten championship golf courses, including The Bear Trace at Cumberland Mountain State Park, Tennessee's first Jack Nicklaus-designed course. Not only will you get your game on in Crossville, but you will also find outdoor activities to keep you busy. Visit Cumberland Mountain State Park to camp overnight, or just plan a day trip. Growing up in Spring City, Crossville is only half an hour away, so we spent a lot of our time going up the mountain to Crossville to shop at the Vanity Fair outlet or to camp at the amazingly beautiful Cumberland Mountain State Park. For some extra camping fun, try reserving a spot for Halloween weekend, when the park is transformed into the biggest trick-or-treat event around! At the park, you'll find a great restaurant, numerous day trails, fishing, paddle-boating, canoeing, kayaking, and paddle-boarding. While you are in Crossville, plan to visit Ozone Falls; this 100 foot falls was so breathtaking that Disney decided to use it in their filming of "The

>TOURIST

Jungle Book". After all of your adventures in Crossville, pop in to one of these favorite local restaurants: Forte's Restaurant on the Square, Homestead Harvest Restaurant, or The Pour House Bistro and Winebar.

25. CHICKAMAUGA AND CHATTANOOGA NATIONAL MILITARY PARK

Chattanooga was known as the "Gateway to the South" during the American Civil War, and this National Military Park lets you walk the history of the battle between the Union and Confederates for control of Chattanooga. There are guided tours, or there are numerous trails and other outdoor activities to help you tour the area at your own pace. Outdoor activities include: hiking, biking, horseback riding, rock climbing, paddling, and picnicking. If you are a history or American Civil War buff, you might also like to visit the four Civil War cemeteries in Chattanooga: Chattanooga National Cemetery (located in downtown Chattanooga), Silverdale Cemetery (located off of Lee Highway right off of Interstate 75), Citizens Cemetery (located across from the University of Tennessee's campus and consists of citizens and Confederate soldiers), and the Forest Hills Cemetery (located at the base of Lookout Mountain in St. Elmo).

26. CARTER HOUSE & CARNTON, FRANKLIN, TN

Visit these historic sites of the Battle of Franklin during the American Civil War. You will get a rarely heard slice of history as you tour both homes and the battlefield. This battle is one not often mentioned, but a crucial one to the outcome of the war. Imagine this private home, Canton, being thrown into a battlefield and hospital in a matter of a few hours. The scars and evidence of the battle still remain on the house. After your trip through history, you are probably ready for some noshing. For finer dining, try: Red Pony Restaurant, Cork & Cow, or Stoney River Steakhouse. For local eats, try: 55 South, Puckett's Gro. and Restaurant, or GRAYS on Main. Franklin's best eats on a budget would take you to: Cool Cafe, 5 Daughters Bakery, Big Shake's Hot Chicken & Fish, or Pasta and Cream.

>TOURIST

27. FORT PILLOW STATE PARK, HENNING

Located about 40 miles north of Memphis and overlooking The Mississippi River, you will find this state park and a whole lot of history. This area of land was a strategic area for battles during the American Civil War, as its steep bluffs and view of The Mississippi River made for great visibility. This state park offers RV camping, primitive camping, and backcountry camping. Outdoor activities such as paddling, boating, hiking, and fishing are available as well as a museum and restored fortifications. Fun history fact: Henning is the hometown of Alex Haley, the author of <u>Roots</u>.

28. KNOXVILLE, THE HEART AND SOUL OF EAST TENNESSEE

The skyline of Knoxville is recognizable by the 266 foot Sunsphere, which was the symbol for the 1982 World's Fair. You can still go to the top of the Sunsphere and enjoy a breathtaking view of the city from the Observation Deck on the 4th floor. Knoxville is home of the college football team The Tennessee Vols. Check out the city during game time for some fun, bustling activity! Downtown Knoxville is beautifully restored and offers over 80 restaurants and 40 boutique shops as well as hosting numerous events throughout the year. If you or any of your travelers are a fan of animals, you must check out the Knoxville Zoo. For a historic stop on your visit, swing by the Mabry-Hazen House, which is listed on the National Register of Historic Places. This beautiful piece of history is now a museum housing over 2,000 original artifacts from the 1800s. Enjoy some local food at one of these eateries: Corner 16, Nick & J's Cafe, Brown Bag, or Stock and Barrel. For the beer connoisseur, stop by: Twisted Mike's Tap Room, Pretentious Beer Co., Harrogate Lounge, Bearden Brickyard, Tapp'd, Sunspot, or Balter Beerworks.

29. BRISTOL, HOME OF THE BRISTOL MOTOR SPEEDWAY

Just one of Bristol's claims to fame is the Bristol Motor Speedway, a legendary NASCAR short-track. After you visit the famous speedway, make your way over to the Birthplace of Country Music Museum for a taste of the historic beginnings of country music. Complete your trip with a visit to their downtown restaurants and shops. A couple restaurants to try when you visit are: Cafe Alona, Baconland BBQ, 620 State, and Old Lighthouse Diner.

30. SUNNY SIDE TRAIL

Up for a Sunday drive? Try following the Sunny Side Trail which starts at the foot of the Smoky Mountains and brings you up through the Tennessee Valley. If you stick to the Sunny Side Trail drive, you can stop at its 179 listed locations for little bits of history and fun! Your trip will start in Sevierville with a commemorative bronze statue of Dolly Parton. Some of the stops along the way include the McMahon Indian Mound, the Applewood Farmhouse Restaurant, and the Old Smokey Mountain Moonshine Distillery. You will also get to drive through the scenic and majestic Appalachian Mountains on park of this trail. This drive is the perfect way to experience East Tennessee!

31. KINGSPORT

One of the Tri-cities, Kingsport hosts a plethora of outdoor activities due to its beautiful scenery. To quench your outdoor thirst, visit one (or all!) of these fun outdoor adventures: Bays Mountain Park and Planetarium, Bays Mountain Adventure Ropes Course, Greenbelt Linear Park, Historic Downtown Kingsport Heritage Trail, and Warrior's Path State Park. Want a fun way to explore Kingsport? Take the Selfie Trail: find the Selfie Markers at seven different locations around Kingsport and take a selfie, then post it to social media with #CaptureKingsport. Finish off your visit with an Original Long Island Iced Tea; legend has it that in the 1920s during Prohibition, a man named Charles Bishop created this well-known beverage while living on Long Island in Kingsport. Restaurants not to miss in Kingsport are: Phil's Dream Pit, Riverfront Seafood Company, and Mr. Papa's and Beer.

>TOURIST

32. JOHNSON CITY

You may recognize this city's name from its mention in the song "Wagon Wheel," but have you ever visited? Start your visit on the Tweetsie Trail for viewing the beautiful city by walking, running, or biking. Next, check out their local breweries on the Brewly Noted Beer Trail. Finish up that day at a show at the Willow Tree Coffee House and Music Room. Your first stop on your next day in Johnson City should be the Gray Fossil Site and Natural History Museum, which is the only Miocene era dig site in the Appalachian Mountains. This is sure to be a crowd pleaser for those dinosaur and fossil enthusiasts. Places for your tastebuds to enjoy include: Freiburg's, The Firehouse Restaurant, and Scratch Brick Oven Foodworks.

33. AUDUBON ACRES, CHATTANOOGA

For beauty in the midst of a bustling city, plan to check out Audubon Acres, a 130-acre wildlife sanctuary located just off of Interstate 75. There are five miles of hiking trails through this pristine protected sanctuary with many spots to picnic while you are there. You can also visit the Visitor's Center which hosts a gift shop and timeline museum of the land. Audubon Acres is also a beautiful spot for family photos or picnicking. In Fall, there is even a "Pioneer Days" celebration where you can take part in life as it used to be in the pioneer days. Check out number three on the list for other things to see and do in Chattanooga.

34. ANDREW JACKSON'S HERMITAGE, NASHVILLE

Andrew Jackson's Hermitage is one of the top visited attractions in Tennessee. This land is a 1,120-acre National Historic Landmark and is considered to be the most accurately preserved early presidential home in the country. There are a variety of tours to choose from including an in-character interpreter to show you through the mansion. Included in the tours, you will also be able to walk through the gardens and farmland of the hermitage. You can visit the tomb of Andrew Jackson and his wife Rachel, which is located in the gardens.

\>TOURIST

35. GAYLORD OPRYLAND HOTEL, NASHVILLE

Book a few nights at the Opryland Hotel and feel as if you have all you need without ever leaving the building. The Opryland Hotel is the largest non-gaming hotel in the continental US and you will feel miles from home in the gorgeous place. There are more than 50,000 tropical plants inside the building along the walking paths of the inner area of the hotel as well as nine acres of waterfalls. You get the pleasure of the outdoors without stepping foot outside. The entertainment, food, nightlife, and dining will keep you fed and happy for your entire stay. You will not be bored with the food selection within the hotel; there are bars, taverns, coffee shops, dessert shops, and steakhouses. There is a fun boat ride on the waterways which snakes through the hotel in which you can experience the botanicals from a whole different perspective. New to Opryland is an indoor/outdoor water park, so be sure to pack your swimsuits! Don't forget about all the fun shops located in the center of the hotel as well. Try to visit during the winter months for a truly spectacular display of lights and decorations. My favorite time to visit is in November to get into the holiday spirit. With the Opry Mills Mall right next door, you can also knock out your holiday shopping at over 200 stores. There are also plenty of fun things to do with the kiddos in the winter months; located outside of the Opryland hotel are an ice skating rink and a snow-tubing arena.

36. THE CAVERNS "PERFORMANCE HALL," PELHAM

Want to hear a concert with the most unique acoustics your ears have ever heard? Grab some tickets to The Caverns, a music venue located in caverns at the base of Monteagle Mountain. If you love bluegrass, you will want to get your tickets for the annual Bluegrass Underground concert. There is only one restaurant in Pelham, Simply Southern, which serves excellent Southern cuisine. If you want more choices, you will want to stop on your way in or out while you are in Monteagle.

>TOURIST

37. CUMBERLAND CAVERNS

Located in McMinnville, Cumberland Caverns is 35 miles of caving adventures. From the inexperienced to the experienced caver, you can choose your adventure ranging from guided walking tours to more advanced and even overnight adventures. Cumberland Caverns can be enjoyed all year round! If you plan on making a day out of it, stop in to one of these restaurants: Collins River BBQ & Cafe, Depot Bottom Country Store, Nana's Kountry Kupboard, Bonnie Blue Inn, or Foutch's Family Restaurant.

38. GRACELAND MANSION

Graceland Mansion is the former home of Elvis Presley and is located in Memphis on a 13.8 acre estate. Tour his house for the day, or get the experience of a lifetime and stay at the Four-Diamond Guest House at Graceland Resort. In addition to touring the mansion, you will also be able to visit museums, exhibits, and Elvis' private jets. Surrounding Graceland, you will find diners and BBQ restaurants galore, so go hungry!

39. ELKMONT CAMPGROUND

Elkmont Campground is located in Gatlinburg, TN and is one of the most popular camping spots. There are many reasons that this campground is so popular, ranging from the 800 miles of maintained hiking trails rated easy to hard, backcountry fishing in The Little River, bear sightings (over 1,500 bears call this area home), and over 90 historic log buildings. One of the most favored trails is one which leads to Laurel Falls, an exquisite 80 foot waterfall. Added bonus: if you can book your trip for the second week of June, you will get to experience the astonishing lightshow of the Fireflies of the Great Smoky Mountains. This is a phenomenal natural event which should be on your bucket list. If you are staying at the campground, you are granted access to the event without needing to enter a lottery in hopes of viewing this natural wonder.

>TOURIST

40. THE BELL WITCH CAVE

Located on the property of the Bell Farm in Adams, Tennessee, The Bell Witch Cave is quite possibly the creepiest place Tennessee has to offer. The Bell Witch is a southern folklore which entails a witch who haunted the Bell family and did horrendous things to them. It is even said that Andrew Jackson was scared off of the property while visiting to try to understand the family's ailments. You can visit the cave and the Bell family's cabin during the months of May through the very end of October. If you are not too spooked to eat, try Adams Station, a small BBQ place worth the stop.

41. VIRGIN FALLS POCKET WILDERNESS

In Sparta, you will find a great place to enjoy some of the most beautiful natural landforms that you could imagine all in one spot. You can choose to hike an eight mile round trip to visit Virgin Falls, a 110 foot cascading falls and even put up your tent along the way to extend your adventure. There are sinkholes, two other waterfalls, and caves to explore as well as a dramatic view off of The Caney Fork Overlook where you will see Scott's Gulf and The Caney Fork River 900 feet below. While in Sparta, bring your appetite and stop at Yanni's Grille, which serves a little of everything. In the mood for something sweet? Go over to C & H Donuts to taste the best in donuts.

42. CASEY JONES VILLAGE

Located in Jackson, you can visit the well-known train enthusiast's house and museum. Casey Jones became a legend when he met a tragic death on his most beloved machine, a locomotive. This village is dedicated to his life and the railroad industry. You can visit his home, a railroad museum, an Old Country Store, an ice cream shop, and a gift store. For great eats in Jackson, try out: Old Town Spaghetti Store, Chandelier Cafe, Latham's Meat Co., or Baker's Rack.

>TOURIST

43. INTERNATIONAL TOWING AND RECOVERY MUSEUM

In 1916, the first tow truck was invented in Chattanooga. This museum honors the evolution of the tow truck and the memories of those who have lost their lives in the service of recovery. Not your average museum, but an interesting one to visit to fully appreciate towing and recovery! A must see for anyone who loves the historical stories behind seemingly everyday operations.

44. PRESIDENT JAMES K. POLK TOMB

President James K. Polk's tomb is not located in a special cemetary or monument, but rather, it's located right in the heart of the capitol in Nashville. Why in Nashville? That's where Polk began his political career. He and his wife, Sarah, are buried only 300 feet away from a statue of President Andrew Jackson, who was a mentor to Polk.

45. BILLY TRIPP'S MINDFIELD

Go just 60 miles Northeast of Memphis to Brownsville to visit the largest outdoor sculpture in Tennessee. The sculpture, an ongoing work of art which Billy Tripp began in 1989, is over an acre large and 125 feet at its tallest. The sculpture is a work of art depicting Billy Tripp's emotions, personal growth, and significant life events. Billy Tripp has even said that upon his death, he will be interred as part of the sculpture. While the town may not be that big, the food is! Try the Mindfield Grill, Brownsville Family Restaurant, Helen's BBQ, or Brownsville Burger Basket.

46. PINSON MOUNDS STATE ARCHEOLOGICAL PARK

A visit to Madison County will bring you to a park dotted with many geographical features which were originally shaped by Native Americans in the Middle Woodland period, roughly 2,000 years ago. Most of the structures take the shape of a mound. These mounds served many purposes, such as burial mounds, ceremonial mounds, or living structures. There have been numerous excavations of some of the mounds in which you can see some artifacts, learn the history, and look back 2,000 years when you visit the museum at the park. If you leave hungry, stop by Snookum's Beef House for some good eats.

47. LOOKOUT MOUNTAIN INCLINE RAILWAY

Located in Chattanooga, you can literally ride above the clouds as this historical railway takes you one mile up the steep side of Lookout Mountain. At its steepest, you will be at an incline of 72.7 percent! You will travel the historic American Civil War path to the site of the "Battle Above the Clouds." When you reach the top, you can stroll around Point Park, visit the little gift shop, and have one of the most breathtaking views of Tennessee that you could imagine.

48. BACKYARD TERROR'S DINOSAUR PARK

Tucked away in rural Tennessee's Bluff City, you will stumble across a fun park filled with homemade lifesize replicas of your favorite childhood creatures: the dinosaurs. This self-guided, donations-only park offers you the most realistic looking dinosaurs in the US. There is even an interactive fossil dig site along the path. After looking at all those dinosaurs, you may have worked up an appetite; stop at Boomershine's Pizzaria, Bluff City Diner, or Ridgewood Barbeque.

49. NATIONAL CIVIL RIGHTS MUSEUM

A true place in history, the site where Martin Luther King, Jr. was shot in 1968, the Lorraine Motel, now functions as the National Civil Rights Museum. Located in Memphis, you can walk the historical timeline of civil rights. The Lorraine Motel has a long history; during segregation, the hotel served high-end visitors such as Ray Charles, Aretha Franklin, and

Otis Redding before the ill-fated and untimely assassination of Martin Luther King, Jr. When I visited this spot, I was overcome with emotions; it is a must-see on your trip to Memphis. Look back at Number 5 on the list for some other places to stop while in Memphis.

50. CONCRETE PARTHENON

Visit the replica of Athens' Parthenon here in Nashville, Tennessee! Located in Nashville's Centennial Park and created out of all concrete, it is considered to be one of the top five art museums in the city. The Parthenon also has an impressive 42 foot replica statue of Athena. This is not all you will find to enjoy at Centennial Park; you can take a quiet meditation in the sunken gardens, walk the mile track around Lake Watauga, take the kids to the playground, or enjoy the volleyball courts. There is also a park band shell which you might be lucky enough to visit during one of their children's theater performances, outdoor movies and concerts, or one of the Shakespeare in the Park plays. Wartime memorabilia from the Spanish-American war also are displayed around the park. Centennial Park was one of my favorite places to visit, as it was located at the backdoor of my college in Murfreesboro.

>TOURIST

TOP REASONS TO BOOK THIS TRIP

Scenic: Experience the most scenic natural beauty in the South.

Outdoor adventure: Take time to enjoy nature and try something new.

Southern Culture: Southern hospitality at its finest.

>TOURIST

BONUS BOOK

50 THINGS TO KNOW ABOUT PACKING LIGHT FOR TRAVEL

PACK THE RIGHT WAY EVERY TIME

AUTHOR: MANIDIPA BHATTACHARYYA

First Published in 2015 by Dr. Lisa Rusczyk. Copyright 2015. All Rights Reserved. No part of this publication may be reproduced, including scanning and photocopying, or distributed in any form or by any means, electronic or mechanical, or stored in a database or retrieval system without prior written permission from the publisher.

Disclaimer: The publisher has put forth an effort in preparing and arranging this book. The information provided herein by the author is provided "as is". Use this information at your own risk. The publisher is not a licensed doctor. Consult your doctor before engaging in any medical activities. The publisher and author disclaim any liabilities for any loss of profit or commercial or personal damages resulting from the information contained in this book.

Edited by Melanie Howthorne

ABOUT THE AUTHOR

Manidipa Bhattacharyya is a creative writer and editor, with an education in English literature and Linguistics. After working in the IT industry for seven long years she decided to call it quits and follow her heart instead. Manidipa has been ghost writing, editing, proof reading and doing secondary research services for many story tellers and article writers for about three years. She stays in Kolkata, India with her husband and a busy two year old. In her own time Manidipa enjoys travelling, photography and writing flash fiction.

Manidipa believes in travelling light and never carries anything that she couldn't haul herself on a trip. However, travelling with her child changed the scenario. She seemed to carry the entire world with her for the baby on the first two trips. But good sense prevailed and she is again working her way to becoming a light traveler, this time with a kid.

INTRODUCTION

*He who would travel happily
must travel light.*

-Antoine de Saint-Exupéry

Travel takes you to different places from seas and mountains to deserts and much more. In your travels you get to interact with different people and their cultures. You will, however, enjoy the sights and interact positively with these new people even more, if you are travelling light.

When you travel light your mind can be free from worry about your belongings. You do not have to spend precious vacation time waiting for your luggage to arrive after a long flight. There is be no chance of your bags going missing and the best part is that you need not pay a fee for checked baggage.

People who have mastered this art of packing light will root for you to take only one carry-on, wherever you go. However, many people can find it really hard to pack light. More so if you are travelling with children. Differentiating between "must have" and "just in case" items is the starting point. There will be ample shopping avenues at your destination which are just waiting to be explored.

This book will show you 'packing' in a new 'light' – pun intended – and help you to embrace light packing practices for all of your future travels.

Off to packing!

DEDICATION

I dedicate this book to all the travel buffs that I know, who have given me great insights into the contents of their backpacks.

THE RIGHT TRAVEL GEAR

1. CHOOSE YOUR TRAVEL GEAR CAREFULLY

While selecting your travel gear, pick items that are light weight, durable and most importantly, easy to carry. There are cases with wheels so you can drag them along – these are usually on the heavy side because of the trolley. Alternatively a backpack that you can carry comfortably on your back, or even a duffel bag that you can carry easily by hand or sling across your body are also great options. Whatever you choose, one thing to keep in mind is that the luggage itself should not weigh a ton, this will give you the flexibility to bring along one extra pair of shoes if you so desire.

2. CARRY THE MINIMUM NUMBER OF BAGS

Selecting light weight luggage is not everything. You need to restrict the number of bags you carry as well. One carry-on size bag is ideal for light travel. Most carriers allow one cabin baggage plus one purse, handbag or camera bag as long as it slides under the seat in front. So technically, you can carry two items of luggage without checking them in.

3. PACK ONE EXTRA BAG

Always pack one extra empty bag along with your essential items. This could be a very light weight duffel bag or even a sturdy tote bag which takes up minimal space. In the event that you end up buying a lot of souvenirs, you already have a handy bag to stuff all that into and do not have to spend time hunting for an appropriate bag.

I'm very strict with my packing and have everything in its right place. I never change a rule. I hardly use

*anything in the hotel room. I wheel my
own wardrobe in and that's it.*

Charlie Watts

CLOTHES & ACCESSORIES

4. PLAN AHEAD

Figure out in advance what you plan to do on your trip. That will help you to pick that one dress you need for the occasion. If you are going to attend a wedding then you have to carry formal wear. If not, you can ditch the gown for something lighter that will be comfortable during long walks or on the beach.

5. WEAR THAT JACKET

Remember that wearing items will not add extra luggage for your air travel. So wear that bulky jacket that you plan to carry for your trip. This saves space and can also help keep you warm during the chilly flight.

6. MIX AND MATCH

Carry clothes that can be interchangeably used to reinvent your look. Find one top that goes well with a couple of pairs of pants or skirts. Use tops, shirts and jackets wisely along with other accessories like a scarf or a stole to create a new look.

7. CHOOSE YOUR FABRIC WISELY

Stuffing clothes in cramped bags definitely takes its toll which results in wrinkles. It is best to carry wrinkle free, synthetic clothes or merino tops. This will eliminate the need for that small iron you usually bring along.

8. DITCH CLOTHES PACK UNDERWEAR

Pack more underwear and socks. These are the things that will give you a fresh feel even if you do not get a chance to wear fresh clothes. Moreover these are easy to wash and can be dried inside the hotel room itself.

9. CHOOSE DARK OVER LIGHT

While picking your clothes choose dark coloured ones. They are easy to colour coordinate and can last longer before needing a wash. Accidental food spills and dirt from the road are less visible on darker clothes.

10. WEAR YOUR JEANS

Take only one pair of Jeans with you, which you should wear on the flight. Remember to pick a pair that can be worn for sightseeing trips and is equally eloquent for dinner. You can add variety by adding light weight cargoes and chinos.

11. CARRY SMART ACCESSORIES

The right accessory can give you a fresh look even with the same old dress. An intelligent neck-piece, a couple of bright scarves, stoles or a sarong can be used in a number of ways to add variety to your clothing. These light weight beauties can double up as a nursing cover, a light blanket, beach wear, a modesty cover for visiting places of worship, and also makes for an enthralling game of peek-a-boo.

12. LEARN TO FOLD YOUR GARMENTS

Seasoned travellers all swear by rolling their clothes for compact and wrinkle free packing. Bundle packing, where you roll the clothes around a central object as if tying it up, is also a popular method of compact and wrinkle free packing. Stacking folded clothes one on top of another is a big no-no as it makes creases extreme and they are difficult to get rid of without ironing.

13. WASH YOUR DIRTY LAUNDRY

One of the ways to avoid carrying loads of clothes is to wash the clothes you carry. At some places you might get to use the laundry services or a Laundromat but if you are in a pinch, best solution is to wash them yourself. If that is the plan then carrying quick drying clothes is highly recommended, which most often also happen to be the wrinkle free variety.

14. LEAVE THOSE TOWELS BEHIND

Regular towels take up a lot of space, are heavy and take ages to dry out. If you are staying at hotels they will provide you with towels anyway. If you are travelling to a remote place, where the availability of towels look doubtful, carry a light weight travel towel of viscose material to do the job.

15. USE A COMPRESSION BAG

Compression bags are getting lots of recommendation now days from regular travellers. These are useful for saving space in your luggage when you have to pack bulky dresses. While packing for the return trip, get help from the hotel staff to arrange a vacuum cleaner.

FOOTWEAR

16. PUT ON YOUR HIKING BOOTS

If you have plans to go hiking or trekking during your trip, you will need those bulky hiking boots. The best way to carry them is to wear them on flight to save space and luggage weight. You can remove the boots once inside and be comfortable in your socks.

17. PICKING THE RIGHT SHOES

Shoes are often the bulkiest items, along with being the dainty if you are a female. They need care and take up a lot of space in your luggage. It is advisable therefore to pick shoes very carefully. If you plan to do a lot of walking and site seeing, then wearing a pair of comfortable walking shoes are a must. For more formal occasions you can carry durable, light weight flats which will not take up much space.

18. STUFF SHOES

If you happen to pack a pair of shoes, ensure you utilize their hollow insides. Tuck small items like rolled up socks or belts to save space. They will also be easy to find.

TOILETRIES

19. STASHING TOILETRIES

Carry only absolute necessities. Airline rules dictate that for one carry-on bag, liquids and gels must be in 3.4 ounce (100ml) bottles or less, and must be packed in a one quart zip-lock bag. If you are planning to stay in a hotel, the basic things will be provided for you. It's best is to buy the rest from the local market at your destination.

20. TAKE ALONG TAMPONS

Tampons are a hard to find item in a lot of countries. Figure out how many you need and pack accordingly. For longer stays you can buy them online and have them delivered to where you are staying.

21. GET PAMPERED BEFORE YOU TRAVEL

Some avid travellers suggest getting a pedicure and manicure just the day before travelling. This not only gives you a well kept look, you also save the trouble of packing nail polish. Remember, every little bit of weight reduced adds up.

ELECTRONICS

22. LUGGING ALONG ELECTRONICS

Electronics have a large role to play in our lives today. Most of us cannot imagine our lives away from our phones, laptops or tablets. However while travelling, one must consider the amount of weight these electronics add to our luggage. Thankfully smart phones come along with all the essentials tools like a camera, email access, picture editing tools and more. They are smart to the point of eliminating the need to carry multiple gadgets. Choose a smart phone that suits all your requirements and travel with the world in your palms or pocket.

23. REDUCE THE NUMBER OF CHARGERS

If you do travel with multiple electronic devices, you will have to bear the additional burden of carrying all their chargers too. Check if a single charger can be used for multiple devices. You might also consider investing in a pocket charger. These small devices support multiple devices while keeping you charged on the go.

>TOURIST

24. TRAVEL FRIENDLY APPS

Along with smart phones come numerous apps, which are immensely helpful in our travels. You name it and you have an app for it at hand – take pictures, sharing with friends and family, torch to light dark roads, maps, checking flight/train times, find hotels and many other things. Use these smart alternatives to traditional items like books to eliminate weight and save space.

I get ideas about what's essential when packing my suitcase.

-Diane von Furstenberg

TRAVELLING WITH KIDS

25. BRING ALONG THE STROLLER

Kids might enjoy walking for a while but they soon tire out and a stroller is the just the right thing for them to rest in while you continue your tour. Strollers also double duty as a luggage carrier and shopping bag holder. Remember to pick a light weight, easy to handle brand of stroller. Better yet, find out in advance if you can rent a stroller at your destination.

26. BRING ONLY ENOUGH DIAPERS FOR YOUR TRIP

Diapers take up a lot of space and add to the weight of your luggage. Therefore it is advisable to carry just enough diapers to last through the trip and a few for afterwards, till you buy fresh stock at your destination. Unless of course you are travelling to a really remote area, in which case you have no choice but to carry the load. Otherwise diapers are something you will find pretty easily.

27. TAKE ONLY A COUPLE OF TOYS

Children are easily attracted by new things in their environment. While travelling they will find numerous 'new' objects to scrutinize and play with. Packing just one favorite toy is enough, or if there is no favorite toy leave out all of them in favor of stories or imaginary games.

28. CARRY KID FRIENDLY SNACKS

Create a small snack counter in your bag to store away quick bites for those sudden hunger pangs. Depending on the child's age this could include chocolates, raisins, dry fruits, granola bars or biscuits. Also keep a bottle of water handy for your little one.

>TOURIST

These things do not add much weight and can be adjusted in a handbag or knapsack.

29. GAMES TO CARRY

Create some travel specific, imaginary games if you have slightly grown up children, like spot the attractions. Keep a coloring book and colors handy for in-flight or hotel time. Apps on your smart phone can keep the children engaged with cartoons and story books. Older children are often entertained by games available on phones or tablets. This cuts the weight of luggage down while keeping the kids entertained.

30. LET THE KIDS CARRY THEIR LOAD

A good thing is to start early sharing of responsibilities. Let your child pick a bag of his or her choice and pack it themselves. Keep tabs on what they are stuffing in their bags by asking if they will be using that item on the trip. It could start out being just an entertainment bag initially but with growing years they will learn to sort the useful from the superfluous. Children as little as four can maneuver a small trolley suitcase like a pro- their experience in pull along toys credit. If you are worried that you may be pulling it for them, you may want to start with a backpack.

31. DECIDE ON LOCATION FOR CHILDREN TO SLEEP

While on a trip you might not always get a crib at your destination, and carrying one will make life all the more difficult. Instead call ahead to see if there are any cribs or roll out beds for children. You may even put blankets on the floor. Weave them a story about camping and they will gladly sleep without any trouble.

32. GET BABY PRODUCTS DELIVERED AT YOUR DESTINATION

If you are absolutely paranoid about not getting your favourite variety of diaper or brand of baby food, check out online stores like amazon.com for services in your destination city. You can buy things online ahead of your travel and get them delivered to your hotel upon arrival.

33. FEEDING NEEDS OF YOUR INFANTS

If you are travelling with a breastfed infant, you save the trouble of carrying bottles and bottle sanitization kits. For special food, or medications, you may need to call ahead to make sure you have a refrigerator where you are staying.

34. FEEDING NEEDS OF YOUR TODDLER

With the progression from infancy to toddler, their dietary requirements too evolve. You will have to pack some snacks for travelling time. Fresh fruits and vegetables can be purchased at your destination. Most of the cities you travel to in whichever part of the world, will have baby food products and formulas, available at the local drug-store or the supermarket.

35. PICKING CLOTHES FOR YOUR BABY

Contrary to popular belief, babies can do without many changes of clothes. At the most pack 2 outfits per day. Pack mix and match type clothes for your little one as well. Pick things which are comfortable to wear and quick to dry.

36. SELECTING SHOES FOR YOUR BABY

Like outfits, kids can make do with two pairs of comfortable shoes. If you can get some water resistant shoes it will be best. To expedite drying wet shoes, you can stuff newspaper in them then wrap them with newspaper and leave them to dry overnight.

37. KEEP ONE CHANGE OF CLOTHES HANDY

Travelling with kids can be tricky. Keep a change of clothes for the kids and mum handy in your purse or tote bag. This takes a bit of space in your hand luggage but comes extremely handy in case there are any accidents or spills.

38. LEAVE BEHIND BABY ACCESSORIES

Baby accessories like their bed, bath tub, car seat, crib etc. should be left at home. Many hotels provide a crib on request, while car seats can be borrowed from friends or rented. Babies can be given a bath in the hotel sink or even in the adult bath tub with a little bit of water. If you bring a few bath toys, they can be used in the bath, pool, and out of water. They can also be sanitized easily in the sink.

39. CARRY A SMALL LOAD OF PLASTIC BAGS

With children around there are chances of a number of soiled clothes and diapers. These plastic bags help to sort the dirt from the clean inside your big bag.

These are very light weight and come in handy to other carry stuff as well at times.

PACK WITH A PURPOSE

40. PACKING FOR BUSINESS TRIPS

One neutral-colored suit should suffice. It can be paired with different shirts, ties and accessories for different occasions. One pair of black suit pants could be worn with a matching jacket for the office or with a snazzy top for dinner.

41. PACKING FOR A CRUISE

Most cruises have formal dinners, and that formal dress usually takes up a lot of space. However you might find a tuxedo to rent. For women, a short black dress with multiple accessory options will do the trick.

42. PACKING FOR A LONG TRIP OVER DIFFERENT CLIMATES

The secret packing mantra for travel over multiple climates is layering. Layering traps air around your body creating insulation against the cold. The same light t-shirt that is comfortable in a warmer climate can be the innermost layer in a colder climate.

REDUCE SOME MORE WEIGHT

43. LEAVE PRECIOUS THINGS AT HOME

Things that you would hate to lose or get damaged leave them at home. Precious jewelry, expensive gadgets or dresses, could be anything. You will not require these on your trip. Leave them at home and spare the load on your mind.

44. SEND SOUVENIRS BY MAIL

If you have spent all your money on purchasing souvenirs, carrying them back in the same bag that you brought along would be difficult. Either pack everything in another bag and check it in the airport or get everything shipped to your home. Use an international carrier for a secure transit, but this could be more expensive than the checking fees at the airport.

45. AVOID CARRYING BOOKS

Books equal to weight. There are many reading apps which you can download on your smart phone or tab.

Plus there are gadgets like Kindle and Nook that are thinner and lighter alternatives to your regular book.

CHECK, GET, SET, CHECK AGAIN

46. STRATEGIZE BEFORE PACKING

Create a travel list and prepare all that you think you need to carry along. Keep everything on your bed or floor before packing and then think through once again – do I really need that? Any item that meets this question can be avoided. Remove whatever you don't really need and pack the rest.

47. TEST YOUR LUGGAGE

Once you have fully packed for the trip take a test trip with your luggage. Take your bags and go to town for window shopping for an hour. If you enjoy your hour long trip it is good to go, if not, go home and reduce the load some more. Repeat this test till you hit the right weight.

48. ADD A ROLL OF DUCT TAPE

You might wonder why, when this book has been talking about reducing stuff, we're suddenly asking you to pack something totally unusual. This is because when you have limited supplies, duct tape is immensely helpful for small repairs – a broken bag, leaking zip-lock bag, broken sunglasses, you name it and duct tape can fix it, temporarily.

49. LIST OF ESSENTIAL ITEMS

Even though the emphasis is on packing light, there are things which have to be carried for any trip. Here is our list of essentials:

- Passport/Visa or any other ID

- Any other paper work that might be required on a trip like permits, hotel reservation confirmations etc.

- Medicines – all your prescription medicines and emergency kit, especially if you are travelling with children

- Medical or vaccination records

- Money in foreign currency if travelling to a different country

- Tickets- Email or Message them to your phone

>TOURIST

50. MAKE THE MOST OF YOUR TRIP

Wherever you are going, whatever you hope to do we encourage you to embrace it whole-heartedly. Take in the scenery, the culture and above all, enjoy your time away from home.

On a long journey even a straw weighs heavy.

-Spanish Proverb

>TOURIST

PACKING AND PLANNING TIPS

A Week before Leaving

- Arrange for someone to take care of pets and water plants.
- Stop mail and newspaper.
- Notify Credit Card companies where you are going.
- Change your thermostat settings.
- Car inspected, oil is changed, and tires have the correct pressure.
- Passports and photo identification is up to date.
- Pay bills.
- Copy important items and download travel Apps.
- Start collecting small bills for tips.

Right Before Leaving

- Clean out refrigerator.
- Empty garbage cans.
- Lock windows.
- Make sure you have the proper identification with you.
- Bring cash for tips.
- Remember travel documents.
- Lock door behind you.
- Remember wallet.
- Unplug items in house and pack chargers.

>TOURIST

READ OTHER GREATER THAN A TOURIST BOOKS

Greater Than a Tourist San Miguel de Allende Guanajuato Mexico: 50 Travel Tips from a Local by Tom Peterson

Greater Than a Tourist – Lake George Area New York USA: 50 Travel Tips from a Local by Janine Hirschklau

Greater Than a Tourist – Monterey California United States: 50 Travel Tips from a Local by Katie Begley

Greater Than a Tourist – Chanai Crete Greece: 50 Travel Tips from a Local by Dimitra Papagrigoraki

Greater Than a Tourist – The Garden Route Western Cape Province South Africa: 50 Travel Tips from a Local by Li-Anne McGregor van Aardt

Greater Than a Tourist – Sevilla Andalusia Spain: 50 Travel Tips from a Local by Gabi Gazon

Greater Than a Tourist – Kota Bharu Kelantan Malaysia: 50 Travel Tips from a Local by Aditi Shukla

Children's Book: Charlie the Cavalier Travels the World by Lisa Rusczyk

>TOURIST

> TOURIST

Visit Greater Than a Tourist for Free Travel Tips
http://GreaterThanATourist.com

Sign up for the Greater Than a Tourist Newsletter for discount days, new books, and travel information:
http://eepurl.com/cxspyf

Follow us on Facebook for tips, images, and ideas:
https://www.facebook.com/GreaterThanATourist

Follow us on Pinterest for travel tips and ideas:
http://pinterest.com/GreaterThanATourist

Follow us on Instagram for beautiful travel images:
http://Instagram.com/GreaterThanATourist

>TOURIST

> TOURIST

Please leave your honest review of this book on Amazon and Goodreads. Please send your feedback to GreaterThanaTourist@gmail.com as we continue to improve the series. We appreciate your positive and constructive feedback. Thank you.

>TOURIST

METRIC CONVERSIONS

TEMPERATURE

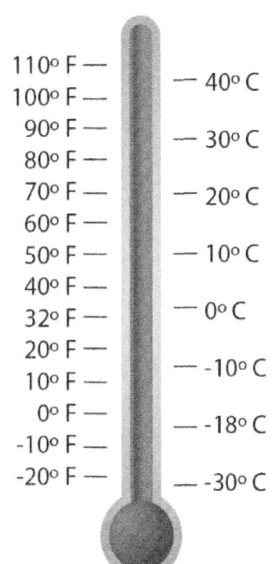

110° F — — 40° C
100° F —
90° F — — 30° C
80° F —
70° F — — 20° C
60° F —
50° F — — 10° C
40° F —
32° F — — 0° C
20° F —
10° F — — -10° C
0° F —
-10° F — — -18° C
-20° F — — -30° C

To convert F to C:

Subtract 32, and then multiply by 5/9 or .5555.

To Convert C to F:
Multiply by 1.8
and then add 32.

32F = 0C

LIQUID VOLUME

To Convert:................Multiply by
U.S. Gallons to Liters............... 3.8
U.S. Liters to Gallons 26
Imperial Gallons to U.S. Gallons 1.2
Imperial Gallons to Liters....... 4.55
Liters to Imperial Gallons 22
1 Liter = .26 U.S. Gallon
1 U.S. Gallon = 3.8 Liters

DISTANCE

To convert ....Multiply by
Inches to Centimeters 2.54
Centimeters to Inches 39
Feet to Meters....................... .3
Meters to Feet 3.28
Yards to Meters 91
Meters to Yards 1.09
Miles to Kilometers 1.61
Kilometers to Miles............ .62
1 Mile = 1.6 km
1 km = .62 Miles

WEIGHT

1 Ounce = .28 Grams
1 Pound = .4555 Kilograms
1 Gram = .04 Ounce
1 Kilogram = 2.2 Pounds

\>TOURIST

TRAVEL QUESTIONS

- Do you bring presents home to family or friends after a vacation?
- Do you get motion sick?
- Do you have a favorite billboard?
- Do you know what to do if there is a flat tire?
- Do you like a sun roof open?
- Do you like to eat in the car?
- Do you like to wear sun glasses in the car?
- Do you like toppings on your ice cream?
- Do you use public bathrooms?
- Did you bring your cell phone and does it have power?
- Do you have a form of identification with you?
- Have you ever been pulled over by a cop?
- Have you ever given money to a stranger on a road trip?
- Have you ever taken a road trip with animals?
- Have you ever went on a vacation alone?
- Have you ever run out of gas?

- If you could move to any place in the world, where would it be?
- If you could travel anywhere in the world, where would you travel?
- If you could travel in any vehicle, which one would it be?
- If you had three things to wish for from a magic genie, what would they be?
- If you have a driver's license, how many times did it take you to pass the test?
- What are you the most afraid of on vacation?
- What do you want to get away from the most when you are on vacation?
- What foods smells bad to you?
- What item do you bring on ever trip with you away from home?
- What makes you sleepy?
- What song would you love to hear on the radio when you're cruising on the highway?
- What travel job would you want the least?
- What will you miss most while you are away from home?
- What is something you always wanted to try?

>TOURIST

- What is the best road side attraction that you ever saw?
- What is the farthest distance you ever biked?
- What is the farthest distance you ever walked?
- What is the weirdest thing you needed to buy while on vacation?
- What is your favorite candy?
- What is your favorite color car?
- What is your favorite family vacation?
- What is your favorite food?
- What is your favorite gas station drink or food?
- What is your favorite license plate design?
- What is your favorite restaurant?
- What is your favorite smell?
- What is your favorite song?
- What is your favorite sound that nature makes?
- What is your favorite thing to bring home from a vacation?
- What is your favorite vacation with friends?
- What is your favorite way to relax?

- Where is the farthest place you ever traveled in a car?
- Where is the farthest place you ever went North, South, East and West?
- Where is your favorite place in the world?
- Who is your favorite singer?
- Who taught you how to drive?
- Who will you miss the most while you are away?
- Who if the first person you will contact when you get to your destination?
- Who brought you on your first vacation?
- Who likes to travel the most in your life?
- Would you rather be hot or cold?
- Would you rather drive above, below, or at the speed limited?
- Would you rather drive on a highway or a back road?
- Would you rather go on a train or a boat?
- Would you rather go to the beach or the woods?

>TOURIST

TRAVEL BUCKET LIST

1.

2.

3.

4.

5.

6.

7.

8.

9.

10.

>TOURIST

NOTES

Printed in Great Britain
by Amazon